The No-Bullying Program

Preventing Bully/Victim Violence at School

Teacher's Manual For Grades 6–8

James Bitney—Curriculum Writer

Beverly B. Title, Ph.D.—Program Developer

JOHNSON INSTITUTE®

Minneapolis

Acknowledgment

The contents of this book are based on the No-Bullying Curriculum model originally developed for the St. Vrain Valley School District, Longmont, Colorado, by Beverly B. Title, with assistance from Lisa Anderson-Goebel, Vivian Bray, K.G. Campanella-Green, Ted Goodwin, Karen Greene, Elizabeth Martinson, Mike O'Connell, and Peggy Stortz.

The Bullying Behavior Chart was developed by Beverly B. Title, Ph.D.; Severance Kelly, M.D.; Louis Krupnik, Ph.D.; Joseph Matthews, M.S.W.; Kendra Bartley, M.A.

Curriculum consultation was provided by Peggy O'Connell.

The No-Bullying Program: Preventing Bully/Victim Violence at School
Teacher's Manual for Grades 6–8

James Bitney, Curriculum Writer

Beverly B. Title, Ph.D., Program Developer

Johnson Institute
7205 Ohms Lane
Minneapolis, Minnesota 55439-2159
612-831-1630 or 800-231-5165

ISBN 1-56246-122-2

Logo design: Diana Garcia

Cover and text design: Crombie Design

Artwork by Sally Brewer Lawrence

Printed in the United States of America

96 97 98 99 / 5 4 3 2 1

CONTENTS

INTRODUCTION
School Zones—Danger Zones

In 1991, 25,000 people were murdered in the United States. During that same year, there were over 67 million handguns in the United States. Sadly, many of the most heavily armed are young people. One official described the arming of America's teenagers as a real "arms race" in which "no one wants to be left behind." Many schools list weapons on campus as one of their top concerns. An eighth grader in a Connecticut junior high school was suspended for refusing to remove his hat. The next day, he came to school with an assault rifle, killed the janitor and wounded the principal and the school secretary.

> A thirteen year old in Florida threatened to torture and kill his social studies teacher after receiving a poor grade on a test. When the boy was arrested, he had two pistols, a box of bullets, and a switchblade.

> After losing a very close foot race, an eighth-grade girl shot the winner, a classmate, in the leg, claiming, "She cheated."

Violence threatens the fiber of our education system both for teachers and for students. In some schools, gun fights have replaced fist fights and "bullet drills" have replaced fire drills. Guns aren't the only weapons at school. Students have been caught with knives, razors, even bombs. Students say they carry weapons for protection. In 1991, over 3 million young people became the victims of violent crime at school.

Teachers do not fare much better than students. A report from the National Education Association indicates that every month of the school year 12% of teachers will have something stolen, 6,000 will have something taken from them forcefully, 120,000 will be threatened, 5,200 will be attacked, and 19% of those attacked will require medical attention.

Violence: A Definition

These startling statistics point out that too many students and teachers are unsafe in their own schools. Too many use violence, witness violence, or are victims of violence. Unfortunately, violence means different things to different people. That is why the Johnson Institute has sought to define violence as:

> **Any word, look, sign, or act that inflicts or threatens to inflict physical or emotional injury or discomfort upon another person's body, feelings, or possessions.**

Violence: A Delineation

Basically, there are two types of violence: peer violence and bully/victim violence.

- *Peer violence* is defined as acts of violence stemming from disagreements, misunderstanding, or conflicting desires among students who are equally matched in strength and power.

- *Bully/victim* violence involves an imbalance of power and strength between students; bully/victim violence occurs whenever a student intentionally, repeatedly, and over time inflicts or threatens to inflict physical or emotional injury or discomfort on another's body, feelings, or possessions.

Both kinds must be dealt with to make our schools safe.

Dealing with Bully/Victim Violence: The No-Bullying Program

Schools can successfully deal with the problem of peer violence by helping students grow in social skills: communication, feeling processing, problem solving, conflict management, and conflict mediation. Unfortunately, schools have not been so successful in dealing with bully/victim violence.

The No-Bullying Program has been designed to provide a research-based, educational model to deal with bully/victim violence in the school. Research has clearly shown that bullies do not respond to social skill work. Bullies do not care that what they are doing is creating problems for others. In fact, they generally enjoy the results of their bullying behavior. The *No-Bullying Program* offers schools a plan for dealing with bullies and bully/victim violence.

Approximately 15% of any school population are bullies or victims of bullies, which means that 85% of the school population are relatively uninvolved in bullying behaviors. To end bullying, the *No-Bullying Program* engages the help of that 85% by:

- clearly defining what is and what is not bullying

- creating empathy for the victims of bullying

- teaching students when and how to report bullying

- establishing clear consequences for bullying that are strictly enforced by everyone in the school

To assure the help of that 85%, the *No-Bullying Program* also insists that *all adults* in the school take more proactive roles in dealing with bullies and their victims. Research has shown that adult intervention is crucial to ending bully/victim violence. Once students realize that reporting bullying to an adult will result in immediate intervention and action (consequences), they feel secure in becoming proactive in ending bullying themselves.

Prior to meeting with the students, you have met with *all* school staff and support staff to:

- overview the *No-Bullying Program* in its entirety

- review research and correct misinformation about bullying: its perpetrators and its victims

- learn how to stop enabling bullying behavior

- agree on a school-wide policy of no-entitlement and no-tolerance with regard to bullying behaviors

- learn intervention strategies with regard to bullying behaviors

- create support networks with community leaders and service providers, professionals in the areas of violence and domestic abuse, law enforcement officials, student leaders, and parent advisory group leaders or members

- establish a procedure enabling the students to feel safe when reporting bullying

- set and commit to the consistent enforcement of school-wide consequences for bullying behaviors

Now, as a teacher, your role in the project is to lead the students through an exciting educational process designed to empower them to end bullying in their school and to make it "Safe Zone" for learning.

HOW TO USE THIS MANUAL

This *Teacher's Manual* offers you material and detailed guidance to lead middle school students (sixth, seventh, and eighth graders) through six 40- to 60-minute sessions of interactive learning. You may lengthen or shorten the session time, depending on the deletion or addition of an activity and your particular teaching style.

You may use this material with sixth, seventh, or eighth graders. However, do not mix grade levels. When you initiate the *No-Bullying Program*, you will no doubt have students in all three grades involved in the sessions. In subsequent years, the majority of the students will be sixth graders. However, you will also need to schedule sessions for seventh and/or eighth graders who are new to your school and/or have never experienced a level of the *No-Bullying Program*.

Aims of the Program

To teach strategically formulated awarenesses and skills that are designed to help the students:

- understand the *No-Bullying Program*

- define bullying, disclose experiences with bully/victim problems, and heighten their awareness of these problems

- better understand bullying, its effects, and the characteristics of those who bully and of their victims

- develop empathy for the victims of bullying

- recognize the distinction between "ratting" and "reporting" in order to get help in a bullying situation

- understand the school-wide consequences for engaging in bullying behaviors

Learning Strategies

The *No-Bullying Program* incorporates a variety of strategies to help you facilitate learning. These strategies include:

- Kinesthetic learning tactics

- Brainstorming

- Drama and role playing

- Group discussion

- Teaching Masters

Kinesthetic Learning Tactics

An ancient Oriental proverb states: "Tell me, I'll forget. Show me, I may remember. But involve me, and I'll understand." Put simply, kinesthetic learning techniques *involve* the students. Using these techniques allows you to appeal to more than one sense of the learner. They even allow you to get learners moving, so that body muscles may respond to the learning stimuli.

When the students hear you say something and, at the same time, see some information you've printed on the board or newsprint, they retain more of what you're saying. As you teach, then, frequently write out words and terms as you say them. Likewise, capture attention by using sight as well as hearing. If you write a word or term, circle, star, box, underline, or check it if you refer to it a second or third time. Draw lines and arrows to connect words—to draw connections between terms. Consider using different colored chalk or markers to show relationships or connections between words and terms. This does more than add color; it makes relationships stand out.

Avail yourself of every opportunity to get the students on their feet, raise their hands, turn in their seats. Encourage them to use all their senses as they learn.

Brainstorming

Brainstorming allows everyone to speak quickly and briefly and puts the burden of knowledge on no one person. Brainstorming is proof of the adage that "All of us are smarter than any one of us." Brainstorming is an activity that's easy to do and with which almost all students are comfortable, since every brainstorming response or idea is an acceptable one.

When the students brainstorm, list their responses (or words that describe them) on the board or newsprint, but don't add your comments; for example: "Good!" "Just what I was thinking." "I don't see how that fits, but I'll write it down anyway." "Do you really mean that?" Your comments, either positive or negative, can prevent some students from saying anything at all or can embarrass others. Be aware that as the students brainstorm, a type of synergism takes place. Initial responses elicit new responses that pull together many ideas into one. This synergism tends to energize the students and make them eager to join in.

When brainstorming, be wary of searching for "the right response" and then stopping the brainstorming once somebody gives it. Instead, set a time limit for brainstorming and get all the responses you can during that time. Or simply end the brainstorming when the students stop coming up with ideas.

Finally, brainstorming helps students realize that they already know a great deal, that the answers to questions they may have already lie within them. Thus brainstorming helps the students value themselves and appreciate that you value them.

Drama and Role Playing

In drama (skits) and role playing, students assume various characters and create roles. During role play, they may explore situations, identify problems, resolve conflicts, and create solutions. In other words, they deal with real-life matters in a safe situation. They can experience a whole range of emotions as they identify with characters and roles and work toward creative solutions. These activities can provide insights for the students that simple discussion cannot.

At the conclusion of a drama (skit) or role play, always offer those who took part the opportunity to express and process their feelings. Likewise offer the observers the chance to share their observations and perceptions.

Group Discussion

In group discussion a synergy that is more than just the sum of the number of students in the group can result from their talking together and sharing ideas. The sum becomes more than the addition of its parts.

Teaching Masters

This level of the *No-Bullying Program* provides you with 20 Teaching Masters (see pages 50–70) which you can reproduce as handouts for the students. The students use them as worksheets to explore the key concepts of a particular session.

Understanding the Pre- and Early Adolescent

For the most part, the following characteristics—all of which are *normal*—are exhibited by the pre- and early adolescent. He or she:

- is beginning to experience bodily and hormonal changes

- needs physical activity to develop physically

- needs to feel and experience that he or she has some ability and can feel confident and successful in some areas

- seeks and requires opportunities to clarify what's important—to clarify goals and values

- is generally too concerned about appearance

- wonders whether he or she will fit in or be accepted by others

- wants to find new avenues of creative expression

- needs positive social interaction with both peers and adults

- often overtly rebels against structures and clear limits, but actually looks for them—counts on them—from adults

- wants and needs to make a real contribution to whatever projects he or she gets involved in

- seeks input into the decisions—big and little—that affect his or her life

- is just beginning to ask bigger questions of meaning and looks to others—peers and adults—as models

Session Components

- **Aim** states the overall goal of the session.

- **Objectives** lists the learning outcomes of the session.

- **Materials** catalogues all the teaching devices necessary to present the session.

- **Preparing for the Session** contains directions for all the pre-session arrangements necessary to present the session.

- **Background for the Teacher** includes pertinent information:

  — to help you set the educational content in context

  — to provide you with added information for personal growth

  — to give you new data necessary to present the session with the greatest success.

- **Session Plan** includes the specific steps or directions for presenting the session. Each **Session Plan** is composed of three parts: *Beginning the Session, Leading the Session,* and *Concluding the Session.*

  — *Beginning the Session* serves to welcome and gather the students, unite them as a group, review previous learning, and get them ready to work and share together.

  — *Leading the Session* includes learning activities, discussions, exercises, drama or role play, as well as other educational processes, presented in a clear, step-by-step design that enables you to guide the students through the session.

  — *Concluding the Session,* which remains relatively the same for every session, includes activities that serve to affirm the students in what they learned during the session and to help them commit themselves to No-Bullying both as individuals and as a school community.

Finally, all of the plans include at least one Optional Activity, which you may choose to use to replace an activity in the plan, to enhance the plan, to extend the session, or to assign as a homework project.

This session plan format strives to give the students a total experience that is structured but hospitable, instructive but creative, and challenging but supportive. Because the format remains constant for each session, it also meets the needs of at-risk students for structure, stability, consistency, and enjoyment. You may use the plans with confidence.

Session 1

Aim

To introduce/review the *No-Bullying Program*

Objectives

By the end of the session, the students will

- recognize and understand the No-Bullying logo

- begin to identify bullying and its effects

- appreciate that their school is committed to ending bullying

Materials

- copy of the No-Bullying logo poster (Teaching Master 1)

- copies of the No-Bullying logos (Teaching Master 2)

- one copy of "A Declaration of Independence from Bullying: Part 1" (Teaching Master 3)

- chalkboard and chalk

- newsprint and markers

- large sheets of construction paper

- scissors, glue sticks

- colored markers

- copies of old magazines

- pens and tape

Preparing for the Session

Carefully read over the session plan in advance. Make a copy of the No-Bullying logo poster (Teaching Master 1) to be used throughout the sessions. Make copies of the No-Bullying logos (Teaching Master 2). Cut out enough logos so that every two students will have one. Then cut the individual logos in half, but in an irregular fashion (like puzzle pieces), so that each fits together only with its matching half. Since you will need more copies of The No-Bullying logos later in the session (see Step 4 below) make enough copies of the sheet so that each work group will have at least one sheet of logos. Have large sheets of construction paper, scissors, glue sticks, colored markers, pens or pencils, and copies of old magazines available. Make one copy of "A Declaration of Independence from Bullying: Part 1" (Teaching Master 3). Decide on an area of the room in which you can conclude this and all future sessions and in which you will be able to post six Teaching Masters. Have pens and tape available. Consider using the Optional Activities.

Background for the Teacher

It is important for you, as a teacher, to understand that bullying is not always obvious. It most often takes place in concealed areas. At school, bullying occurs where you're not present or where you can't see: in bathrooms, in hallways, in areas that are difficult to supervise, in empty classrooms, etc. Simply because you do not witness bullying behaviors does not mean they aren't taking place.

Session Plan

Beginning the Session

Greet the students warmly as they arrive. If necessary, take a moment to introduce yourself to the group. Then give each student a pen or pencil and one of the No-Bullying logo halves you cut and prepared prior to the session. Invite students to write their names on their half logo. Explain to them that their half logo matches someone else's in the group. Direct them to circulate and compare their half logos. When they identify a match, have them pair up with the person who has it, introduce themselves to one another, and then share one thing that makes them feel safe at school. When all students have found their partners, have them introduce one another to the rest of the group and tell what one another said that makes them feel safe at school.

Leading the Session

1. Display the No-Bullying logo poster (Teaching Master 1). Point out to the students how it matches the smaller logos they have. Ask them what they think it means (or what they remember about it from past years). Accept all replies and list on newsprint.

2. Go on to discuss the logo with the group. Encourage the students to share:

   • what types of things they think those who engage in bullying do

   • why they think some kids engage in bullying

   • what happens to those who bully others

   • what happens to victims of bullying

   • how bullying affects their school

   Again, as they discuss, list the students' ideas on newsprint.

3. After the discussion, tell the students that they will be talking more about bullying behavior—about students taking unfair advantage of others—for the next few weeks. Stress that your school is committed to stopping all bullying and getting hurt by bullying in your school. Then say:

   "In our class time together, we will grow in solidarity, learn how to support each other, and discover the best ways to get help to end bullying. However, whenever we talk about bullying *in this class*, we will never call anyone by name who is bullying or being bullied. We will never label anyone a *bully* or a *victim* by name."

4. Divide the students into cooperative work groups. Give each group a large piece of construction paper, a sheet of No-Bullying logos (Teaching Master 2), glue sticks, scissors, colored markers, and copies of magazines. Explain to the groups that they are to use their own art work (drawings/designs) along with pictures and words cut out of the magazines to design a collage poster discouraging bullying. Direct the groups to work together to draw on the results of their discussion (using what's written on the newsprint sheets) in order to depict what types of things they think those who engage in bullying do, what might happen to victims of bullying, and any ways bullying affects their school. Tell the groups that they are to use the No-Bullying logos within their collages to show that they refuse to tolerate bullying in their school.

5. When the groups finish their work, have each present its collage to the class. Afterward, collect the collages and the rest of the art materials. Tell the students that you will post their collages throughout the school.

Note: After the session, and before posting the students' collages, look them over carefully. What the students have depicted can help to give you a picture of how they presently view bullying. You can draw on and build on these perceptions as you present information in the sessions to come.

6. Give the students a "homework" assignment to interview at least three people from their family, friends, and neighbors prior to the next session. Have the students ask those they interview simply to complete the following sentence:

"I think bullying is…"

Tell the students to record the responses along with the sex and age of the person being interviewed. Explain that you will share results in Session 2.

Note: Be sure that *you* do this assignment as well. Interview three people and be ready to share their replies in the next session.

Concluding the Session

Gather the students in an area of the meeting room where you can post all six parts of a Declaration of Independence from Bullying.

Ask the students if they've heard of the United States' Declaration of Independence. Take a moment to remind them that the founders of our nation signed the Declaration of Independence to forge a future that insured the rights of all to life, liberty, and the pursuit of happiness, free from the bullying of a foreign monarchy. Then go on to explain to the students that they are going to have the opportunity to make their own declaration of independence, a declaration of independence from bullying.

Give one of the students a copy of "A Declaration of Independence from Bullying: Part 1" (Teaching Master 3). Ask him or her to read it aloud to the group:

> We, the generation that will be adults in the twenty-first century, in order to grow to be our best selves and to shape a future free of abuse, declare our independence from bullying by saying "No!" to bullying in our school.

After the reading, have the student post the sheet. Then, invite the students to declare their independence from bullying by asking:

- What are some ways we can say say "No!" to bullying in our school?

Accept all responsible ideas. Remind the students of the time of their next session, when they will arrive at a precise definition of bullying behavior and will also take part in an important survey.

Optional Activities

1. Encourage the students to keep a journal. Suggest they use a simple notebook that is "for their eyes only." Recommend that they choose a specific time each day to spend journaling. To get the students started, suggest a couple of journal questions like the following:

   - Why do people bully others?

   - If you have ever been the victim of bullying, how did that treatment make you feel?

   Tell the students to spend time reflecting on the questions and only then to respond to them in writing in their journals.

2. To expand the activity in "Concluding the Session," consider inviting students to sign their names to the copy of "A Declaration of Independence from Bullying: Part 1" (Teaching Master 3).

SESSION 2

Aim

To help the students define bullying, disclose experiences with bully/victim problems, and heighten their awareness of these problems

Objectives

By the end of the session, the students will

- discover a definition of bullying
- understand that bullying involves an imbalance of power and repeated negative action
- share experience of—and become more aware of—bullying and its effects
- better appreciate how their school is committed to ending bullying

Materials

- the No-Bullying logo poster from Session 1
- newsprint and markers
- copy of "A Declaration of Independence from Bullying: Part 1" (Teaching Master 3) from Session 1
- copies of "Bullying Happens…" (Teaching Master 4)
- copies of "What's Happening?" (Teaching Master 5)
- one copy of "A Declaration of Independence from Bullying: Part 2" (Teaching Master 6)
- pens or pencils
- tape

Preparing for the Session

Carefully read through the session plan in advance. Make each student a copy of "Bullying Happens…" (Teaching Master 4). On a sheet of butcher paper as long as the combined widths of three sheets of newsprint, use a marker (or art letters) to print the definition of bullying—from "Bullying Happens…" (Teaching Master 4):

> BULLYING HAPPENS…
>
> **when someone with *greater* power**
>
> *unfairly* **hurts someone**
>
> **with *less* power**
>
> *over and over again.*

Then, with a marker, head separate sheets of newsprint with the following phrases: "Physical Power," "Verbal Power," and "Social Power." (**Note:** If the class is large, consider making two of each of the above sheets, to be used by six, rather than three, small groups—see Step 3 below.) Make each student a copy of the survey "What's Happening?" (Teaching Master 5). Have pens or pencils, markers, and tape (transparent or masking) available. Make one copy of "A Declaration of Independence from Bullying: Part 2" (Teaching Master 6). Consider assigning the Optional Activities. See to it that the No-Bullying logo poster (from Session 1) is prominently displayed in the classroom.

Background for the Teacher

In this session, the students define or label bullying behavior. Although it is clearly judgmental and unfair to attach "labels" to people, it can be very help-ful to label certain behavior. Thus, labeling some behavior as "bullying" can help the students gain valuable insight into that behavior—to see not only the *what* but the *why* of the behavior. Likewise, such labeling also helps students understand that bullying behavior happens "outside" of them and their reac-tions to it. In other words, the students come to recognize that the bullying person acts the way he or she acts not just toward a particular person, but toward all others. Recognizing this helps the students not to take the behavior personally—to understand that it's not their fault—and enables them to gain the necessary distance between themselves and the person engaged in the behavior so that they may be able to deal with bullying effectively. At the same time, this recognition also helps the students grow in empathy toward those who are victims of bullying behavior.

Besides using the survey, "What's Happening?" during this session, feel free to re-use it at any time you feel the need to do a perception check on bullying. Whenever you administer the survey, be sure to share results with other school staff. That way, your school will have a broader perspective on the problem.

Session Plan

Beginning the Session

Display the No-Bullying logo poster. To review Session 1, ask the students to recall the collages they made. Remind the students that whenever they talk about bullying *in class* they should not call anyone by name who may be bullying or being bullied. Then, go on to ask volunteers to offer examples of the following:

- the types of things those who engage in bullying do

- why some kids might engage in bullying

- what happens to victims of bullying

- how bullying affects their school

Leading the Session

1. Review the "homework" interviews assigned in Session 1. To begin, share the responses you received. Then call on different students to share at least one of the responses they got. List on the board or newsprint.

   After getting a representative sampling, invite the students to point out both similarities and differences in the responses to "I think bullying is…" Conclude by telling the students that it is important to agree on a definition of bullying in order to recognize it when it happens and to deal with it effectively.

2. Distribute pens or pencils and copies of the definition of bullying behavior, "Bullying Happens…" (Teaching Master 4). Display the large butcher

paper poster of the definition that you made prior to the session. Call on one of the students to read the definition aloud:

> **BULLYING HAPPENS...**
>
> **when someone with *greater* power**
>
> ***unfairly* hurts someone**
>
> **with *less* power**
>
> *over and over again.*

Point out and use a marker to circle the word "power" in the definition, and ask the students to circle it on their sheets. Then explain to the group that those who engage in bullying behavior use different types of "power" to bully others.

3. Depending on the size of the class, divide the students into three or six groups. Give each group a marker and one of the newsprint "Power" sheets you made prior to the session. Direct each small group to come up with examples of the type of power listed on its "Power" sheet: *Physical Power*, *Verbal Power*, or *Social Power*. Explain that each person in each small group should try to make a contribution. While the small groups are working, circulate and offer help.

   Note: The small group(s) assigned to *Social Power* may need some hints from you to get started. Check in with this group first and, if necessary, offer some examples of social power such as "hurting feelings," "spreading rumors," or "excluding others." Point out that social power can be both physical and verbal.

4. Ask each small group to choose a Reporter to present its ideas to the class. Look for examples like the following:

Physical Power	Verbal Power	Social Power
size	threats	humiliating
hitting	insults	excluding
pushing	name-calling	hurting
stealing	teasing	feelings
defacing/destroying property	making fun of another	playing mean tricks
threatening with a weapon	intimidating phone calls	put-downs gossip/rumors

After each presentation, solicit further ideas from the large group and have the small group Reporter(s) add them to the list.

Finally, help the Reporters use tape to attach their lists to the butcher paper (which contains the definition of bullying), and thus to create a large "Bullying Happens…" poster for the classroom.

Note: You will need this poster for the remainder of the sessions.

5. Call the students' attention to the three columns on their "Bullying Happens…" sheets (Teaching Master 4). Have the students fill in the blanks with the names of the three types of power they just discovered. Then, pointing out the lists on the "Bullying Happens…" poster the students just created, have them copy the examples of behaviors under the appropriate "power" heading on their sheets.

   When the students finish writing, draw attention to the final line in the bullying definition, "over and over again," by using a marker to circle it on the "Bullying Happens…" poster. Direct the students to circle the phrase on their individual sheets. Emphasize to the group that if someone has greater "power" than someone else in any of these three areas and uses that "power" to hurt *over and over again*," such behavior is bullying.

6. Tell the students that now that they have a definition of bullying, they will be completing an important survey about it. Make it clear that the survey is not a test and that it is anonymous. Explain that the survey simply asks them to respond to statements about their life at school. Point out that there are no right or wrong answers and that some of the items may have more than one answer. Tell the students that as they respond to each statement, they should mark as many answers as apply to them.

7. Distribute copies of the survey, "What's Happening?" (Teaching Master 5) and allow the students to complete it on their own.

8. When everyone is finished, help the students better "own" the survey by drawing attention to statement #5 (*I think that most of the bullying that happens at our school happens…*). Then ask the students to raise their hands if they checked the first possible response (*in classrooms*). Have one of the students record the number of responses on the board or newsprint. Do the same for the five remaining possible responses. Finally, have the students count up the responses and determine what they, as a group, believe to be the place(s) in their school where most bullying happens.

9. Go on to repeat the above procedure for statement #10 (*To help me feel safe at school, I think adults should…*). Ask a different student to act as recorder.

Afterward, assure the students that you will convey their concerns about where bullying takes place in their school, what they'd like adults to do about it, as well as all other pertinent information from their surveys to other adults in the school, including the principal.

Finally, collect the surveys and the pens or pencils.

Note: Be sure to review all the surveys prior to the next session, paying particular attention to any information students volunteer on the back of the surveys.

Concluding the Session

Gather the students in the area of the meeting room where you've posted "A Declaration of Independence from Bullying: Part 1" (Teaching Master 3). Ask one of the students to read the poster aloud.

Then give a different student a copy of "A Declaration of Independence from Bullying: Part 2" (Teaching Master 6). Ask him or her to read it aloud to the group:

> *We recognize that bullying is an abuse of power whose negative effects fill our school with fear. We now declare that we say "No!" to bullying and promise to work to make our school a place where no one has to be afraid.*

After the reading, have the student post the sheet. Then invite all the students to declare their independence from bullying by asking:

- What can we do to make our school a place where no one has to feel afraid and say "No!" to bullying in our school?

After the students offer their ideas, thank them for their suggestions and their commitment. Then, before dismissing the group, remind them of the time of their next session, when they will discover even more about bullying and its effects and some of the characteristics of those who bully and of those who are victims of bullying.

Optional Activities

1. If your students are keeping journals, suggest a journal question like the following:

   - If you have bullied someone, why do you think you acted the way you did?

   Remind the students to spend time reflecting on the question before responding in their journals.

2. To expand the activity in "Concluding the Session," consider inviting students to sign their names to the copy of "A Declaration of Independence from Bullying: Part 2" (Teaching Master 6).

3. Have the students look through newspapers or magazines or other references at home to find examples of "Bullies of the World." Examples could include people, countries, or individual acts that victimize others.

   Note: If you choose to use this "homework" activity, be sure to schedule time for sharing at the beginning of the Session 3.

Session 3

Aim

To help the students better understand bullying, its effects, and the characteristics both of those who bully and of their victims

Objectives

By the end of the session, the students will

- become more aware of—by portraying—bullying and its effects

- dispel some of the myths surrounding bullying and its victims

- discover the characteristics of those who bully and of the victims of bullying

Materials

- the No-Bullying logo poster

- the "Bullying Happens…" poster from Session 2

- copies of "A Declaration of Independence from Bullying: Parts 1 & 2" (Teaching Masters 3 & 6)

- copy of the Bullying Behavior chart (see page 69) [For teacher use only.]

- poster paper, newsprint, and markers

- copies of "20 Statements" (Teaching Master 7)

- copies of "The Bully/Victim Characteristics" chart (Teaching Master 8)

- copies of "The Bully/Victim Characteristics" grid (Teaching Master 9)

- one copy of "A Declaration of Independence from Bullying: Part 3" (Teaching Master 10)

- chalkboard and chalk

- newsprint and markers

- writing paper

- pens or pencils

- optional: posterboard

Preparing for the Session

Carefully read through the entire session plan. Make copies of "20 Statements" (Teaching Master 7) and "The Bully/Victim Characteristics" chart (Teaching Master 8), one for each student. Also, make copies of "The Bully/Victim Characteristics" grid (Teaching Master 9), one for every two students. Note that "The Bully/Victim Characteristics" grid (Teaching Master 9), which the students will use in Step 6 below to check on bully and/or victim characteristics presented in small group skits, has been designed to tabulate four small groups. Therefore, if you expect to have more than *four* small groups, you will need to make more copies of Teaching Master 9. Make one copy of "A Declaration of Independence from Bullying: Part 3" (Teaching Master 10). Have pens or pencils available and enough writing paper for half the class.

Make a "Bullying Behaviors" poster by dividing a sheet of posterboard or a large sheet of newsprint into three columns as below:

Bullying Behaviors

Hurting someone's body or things	Hurting someone's feelings	Hurting someone's friendships

If you haven't done so as yet, take time to review the "What's Happening?" surveys the students completed in Session 2 and be ready to offer the students some feedback. Make a copy of the Bullying Behavior chart (see page 69). Review the chart prior to the session and have it handy for your own use as you lead the students through "Beginning the Session" below.

Have markers available. Consider using the Optional Activities. See to it that both the No-Bullying logo poster and the "Bullying Happens..." poster are displayed in the meeting space.

Background for the Teacher

Studies have shown that bullying behaviors include not only forms of physical aggression, but also emotional harassment, social alienation, and both subtle and overt intimidation (the latter often being—but not exclusively—the behavior of girls who engage in bullying). No matter the type, bullying behaviors are usually difficult to detect. However, as a teacher, you need to be aware that all types of bullying occur at school. Likewise, it's also important to remember that bullying behaviors are *learned*. As such, they can be unlearned.

Besides deepening the students' understanding of bullying behaviors, this session also presents the characteristics of those who bully as well as of their victims. The session seeks to dispel some of the myths surrounding bullying; for example, that those who bully have low self-esteem, are all males, or feel guilty about their behavior. It also introduces the students to the plight of bullying's victims, an introduction that will be built upon in successive sessions. As you lead the students through this session, be cautious not to identify or imply by name any students who may be engaging in bullying behaviors or who may be victims of such behavior.

Session Plan

Beginning the Session

Take a moment to get the students settled. Then, invite the group to recall the survey from Session 2. Give the students some feedback about their responses to the survey. You do not have to be particularly specific, but do offer some feedback to let the students know that you appreciate and value their input and honesty. Depending on the students' answers on the survey, you might say:

> "According to the survey, more girls than boys said that they would fight back if they were being bullied. We'll be talking about whether or not this is a good idea."

> or

> "According to the survey, many of you don't really seem to know what to do when you see someone else being bullied. We will be doing some talking and learning about what to do."

Let the students know that their concerns are both valid and important to you. Assure them that you will continue to pass on their concerns to other staff in your school.

Note: If the students took part in Session 2's third Optional Activity (researching "Bullies of the World"), now would be a good time to allow them to share what they discovered.

Leading the Session

1. Display the "Bullying Behaviors" poster you made prior to the session.

Bullying Behaviors

Hurting someone's body or things	Hurting someone's feelings	Hurting someone's friendships

Direct the students to refer to the "Bullying Happens..." poster displayed in the room and to give some examples of how someone might misuse power to engage in behaviors that would fit in each of the "Bullying Behaviors" categories. List the students' ideas under the appropriate headings on the poster.

As the students offer their ideas, use your copy of the Bullying Behavior chart as a referent to recommend other behaviors to add to the poster. Afterward, tell the students that they will be discovering more about such behaviors in this session.

2. Distribute copies of "20 Statements" (Teaching Master 7) and pens or pencils. Read the directions aloud to the students, then have them complete the sheet on their own.

3. When the students are finished marking their sheets, hand out copies of "The Bully/Victim Characteristics" chart (Teaching Master 8). Give the students a moment or two to read through the sheet silently. Then point out that while there are two types of victims of bullying, passive and provocative, both types always have less power than the person who is bullying and neither type ever "deserves" to be bullied.

4. Divide the class into small groups, three to five students per group. Explain that group members are to work together, using the information on "The Bully/Victim Characteristics" chart, to check (and correct) group members' responses on the "20 Statements" sheet.

Afterward, call on different small group members to share responses to the "20 Statements" and to explain (based on the information on "The Bully/Victim Characteristics" chart), why a particular statement is True or False.

Note: For your convenience, the correct responses to the "20 Statements" are included below:

Kids who bully others…

1. **F**   usually feel guilty about their behavior.

2. **T**   don't really feel compassion for others.

3. **F**   are boys only. Girls don't bully.

4. **F**   are loners.

5. **T**   may feel secure and have high self-image.

6. **F**   do not really mean to hurt others.

7. **T**   feel that their victims deserve to be bullied.

8. **T**   usually do okay in school work.

9. **F**   will back off if their victims fight back.

10. **T**   always win.

Kids who are victims of bullying…

1. **F**   usually get what they deserve.

2. **F**   feel secure and have high self-image.

3. **T**   are loners.

4. **T**   sometimes provoke the bullying.

5. **F**   should fight back.

6. **T**   cry easily.

7. **T**   spend a lot of time and energy being afraid.

9. **F**   never carry weapons for protection.

10. **T**   always lose.

As the students explain their responses, take time to gently correct any misunderstandings.

5. Have the students remain in their small groups. Ask them to name favorite television programs—preferably sitcoms (situation comedies). List on the board or newsprint. Explain that each small group will create and perform a sitcom "episode" that illustrates bullying. Have each group select a different sitcom from the list on the board or newsprint. Encourage the small group members to draw on the lists of bullying behaviors found on the "Bullying Happens…" poster and on the characteristics found on "The Bully/Victim Characteristics" chart (Teaching Master 8) as they devise their skit. Emphasize that the students *may not* portray hostile or violent responses toward the bullying behavior. The point of this exercise is illustration, not retaliation. Remind the small groups that each member must contribute in some way to his or her group's presentation. Give the small groups sufficient time to develop their presentations.

6. Before asking the small groups to present their skits, give half the class sheets of writing paper and the other half copies of "The Bully/Victim Characteristics" grid (Teaching Master 9). Tell the class that as each small group presents its skit, those with the blank writing paper are to record any examples of bullying behavior they see portrayed. Those with the copies of "The Bully/Victim Characteristics" grid are to check on the grid any bully and/or victim characteristics they see portrayed.

7. Have the small groups, one at a time, present their sitcom skits to the class. After each presentation, briefly review it by calling on different class members to name the bullying behaviors and the bully/victim characteristics they observed.

Briefly discuss each skit by using questions like the following to focus attention on the bully/victim aspects of each small group presentation:

- What types of feelings did the bullying behaviors generate?

- What behaviors did the victim(s) display?

- Was the victim(s) *passive* or *provocative*?

- How did the skit make you feel toward the character(s) who was bullying?

- How did the skit make you feel toward the character(s) who was the victim(s) of the bullying?

Be sure to compliment the small group members on their presentations and the rest of the class on their observations.

Note: Should any of the skits portray a "Hollywood ending" to a bully/victim situation—for example, a victim physically overpowering a bully—gently question whether such a resolution is likely, given the characteristics of those who bully and those who are victims. Likewise, should any of the skits portray a resolution in which bullying is non-violently foiled by the support of a group and/or the intervention of an adult, be sure to point this out to the students and to explain that they will be learning more about how they, as a group/school, can successfully deal with—and *end*—bullying.

8. After all the skits have been presented and discussed, draw attention to the "Bullying Behaviors" poster used earlier in this session. If the students portrayed/observed other examples of bullying behavior that are not listed on the poster, have them add them now. Tell the students that you will keep this poster displayed in the meeting room for the remainder of their sessions to help them remember what bullying is.

Collect pens/pencils unless you plan to use Optional Activity 2 on page 28.

Concluding the Session

Gather the students in the area of the meeting room where you've posted "A Declaration of Independence from Bullying: Parts 1 & 2" (Teaching Masters 3 & 6). Ask one of the students to read both parts aloud.

Then, give a different student a copy of "A Declaration of Independence from Bullying: Part 3" (Teaching Master 10). Ask him or her to read it aloud to the group:

> We understand that bullying is isolating. It separates us, turning us into perpetrators or victims or observers. It shatters community and changes "all of us" to "them and us." We now declare that we say "No!" to bullying and promise to work to make our school a place where no one has to feel left out.

After the reading, have the student post the sheet. Then, invite them to become independent of bullying by saying:

> "If you are you willing to say 'No!' to bullying in our school by making it a place where no one has to feel left out, please raise your hand."

Go on to encourage those who have raised their hands to suggest ways they can *include* others.

Afterward, thank the students for their commitment and ideas. Then, remind them of the time of their next session, when they will better understand how the victims of bullying feel and discover how victims need our help and support.

Optional Activities

1. If your students are keeping journals, suggest a journal question like the following:

   • Do you agree with the definition of bullying? Why or why not?

   • Do kids who engage in bullying behavior naturally "grow out of it" when they become adults?

   • Do the victims of bullying "get what they deserve"?

2. To expand the activity in "Concluding the Session," consider inviting students to sign their names to the copy of "A Declaration of Independence from Bullying: Part 3" (Teaching Master 10).

3. Challenge the students to work with a partner on a project that examines and reports on instances and types of violence occurring in their community. Sources may include newspaper articles, police reports, and radio and television news programs.

   Note: If you choose to use this "homework" activity, be sure to schedule time for sharing during a subsequent session.

Session 4

Aim

To help the students develop empathy for the victims of bullying

Objectives

By the end of the session, the students will

- recognize the difference between bullying and peer conflict

- better understand how being bullied feels

- realize that victims of bullying need their help

- increase their level of empathy for those victimized by bullying

Materials

- the No-Bullying logo poster

- the "Bullying Happens…" poster

- the "Bullying Behaviors" poster from Session 3

- copies of "A Declaration of Independence from Bullying: Parts 1, 2, & 3" (Teaching Masters 3, 6, & 10)

- one copy of "A Declaration of Independence from Bullying: Part 4" (Teaching Master 12)

- chalkboard and chalk or newsprint and markers

- pens or pencils

- copies of "Is It Bullying?" (Teaching Master 11)

- writing paper

Preparing for the Session

Carefully read through the entire session plan in advance. Make copies of "Is It Bullying?" (Teaching Master 11), one for each student. Make one copy of "A Declaration of Independence from Bullying: Part 4" (Teaching Master 12). Have pens or pencils and writing paper at hand. Throughout the session, be cautious not to identify or imply by name any students who engage in bullying behaviors or who are victims of such behavior.

Give some careful thought to the role play activity outlined in Steps 4 and 5 of the Session Plan. If you feel that your students may have difficulty "portraying" the feelings of the victims of bullying, consider restructuring the activity as follows: Give each small group a copy of the Feelings List (see page 71). Instead of presenting a role play, have small group members choose from the list of feeling words that they think both the "victim" and the "observers" in their scenario may be feeling.

Consider using the Optional Activities. If you choose to employ the third Optional Activity, make all arrangements in advance. Be sure that the No-Bullying logo poster, the "Bullying Happens…" poster, and the "Bullying Behaviors" poster are displayed in the room.

Background for the Teacher

Imagine how you, an adult, would feel if you were being harassed at work or were receiving threatening phone calls or were being stalked by someone. Surely, you'd feel annoyed, upset, angry, frightened, maybe even terrified. Your feelings would spur you to take evasive action to avoid the harassment, the threats, the stalking. You'd look for help. So it is with children who are victims of bullying. These children devote enormous energy to avoid being bullied. Nearly all their activity at school is focused on getting and staying safe. Unfortunately, they cannot put an end to bullying on their own due to the intrinsic imbalance in bully/victim situations. Bullying is a problem its victims cannot solve on their own. They need the help of others. They need and deserve the help of everyone in your school.

This session aims to end bullying and to aid its victims by helping *all* the students learn to understand and empathize with those victims. As you lead the students through this session, take care not to allow their empathy for the victims of bullying to turn to aggression against those who are bullying. The goal is not to avenge victims of bullying, but to help them feel protected and safe at school.

Session Plan

Beginning the Session

Welcome the students as they arrive and give them a moment to get settled. Review the previous session by asking:

- Do you think victims of bullying get what they deserve? (No. No one deserves to be bullied.)

- Do you think victims of bullying are the only ones who can solve the problem of bullying? Why or why not? (No. Victims of bullying are the only ones who *can't* solve the problem of bullying.)

- If they don't get help, do victims of bullying ever win? Why? (No. Never. Because of the inherent imbalance of power.)

Tell the student that in this session they will discover why victims of bullying have the deck stacked against them and why they need help and support in order to put an end to the bullying.

Leading the Session

1. Distribute pens or pencils and copies of "Is It Bullying?" (Teaching Master 11). Go through the directions on the sheet with the students, then allow them time to complete it on their own.

2. Process the activity by calling on volunteers to share responses to the scenarios, one at a time, and to tell whether the scenario portrays bullying. Have each respondent tell *why* or *why not* he or she believes a scenario is a description of bullying.

   Note: Look for recognition that bullying (1) involves an imbalance of power; and (2) *normally* includes some pattern of repetition of behavior. For the purpose of this exercise, the students are encouraged to identify both these characteristics of bullying. Point out, however, that some children who engage in bullying "randomize" their actions—that is, they inflict harm on different victims—in order to avoid detection.

   For your convenience, the correct responses to the scenarios in "Is It Bullying?" (Teaching Master 11) are listed on the next page:

(1) Yes	(6) Yes
(2) Yes	(7) No
(3) No	(8) No
(4) Yes	(9) Yes
(5) No	(10) No

3. Once the students have identified the *bullying* scenarios, take a moment to explain that the other scenarios describe conflict situations that—while including violence—stem from disagreements, misunderstandings, or contested desires between or among students who are *equally matched* in strength and power. The bullying scenarios, on the other hand, involve an imbalance of power and strength between or among students.

4. Divide the students into five small groups. Assign each group one of the bullying scenarios (1, 2, 4, 6, and 9) from "Is It Bullying?" (Teaching Master 11). Direct each small group to use its scenario to develop a role play that demonstrates how the person being bullied *feels*. Tell the small groups that if a scenario calls for only two "players" (the bullying child and the child being bullied), other members of the small group should "play" observers, that is, characters who witness the bullying. In such a role play, the "observers" are to dramatize how *they* feel when they see someone else being bullied. Give the members of the small groups time to develop their role plays.

5. When the students are ready, call on the small groups, one at a time, to present the role plays. After each role play, process it by asking questions like the following:

- What feelings did the person being bullied portray?

- What other feelings do you think the person may have had?

- Do you think that the bullied person had a right to feel that way?

- Would you call those feelings troubled or untroubled?

- How might you feel if something like this happened to you?

- Why would you feel that way? (Expect the students to recognize the unfairness of the bullying behavior.)

- If the role play had "observers" of the bullying behavior, what feelings did they portray?

- How do *you* feel when you see someone else being bullied?

6. After all the role plays have been presented, thank the students for their cooperation and good work. Then sum up the experience by pointing out that victims of bullying feel threatened, alone, frightened, sad, powerless, etc. Write these feelings on the board or newsprint and ask volunteers to mention other troubled feelings bullying victims might have. Conclude by telling the students:

> "When we experience feelings like these, we want to do something about it. We want to change. Students who are victims of bullying can't always make changes on their own. In fact, because they are *in some way always* less powerful than the student who is bullying, victims can never win, can never stand up to bullying on their own. They need help. They need your help and mine. They need the help of *everyone* in our school."

7. Have the students get back into the same small groups they were a part of earlier in this session (see Step 4). Give each small group writing paper and a pen or pencil. Tell the small group members to choose one of the *victims* of bullying they saw portrayed in the role plays—but *not* the victim they portrayed—and, as a group, to write a note of support to that person. Suggest that each small group agree on a "Secretary" who will do the actual writing of the note, but be sure to stress that every member of the small group must contribute to the content of the note. Tell the groups to mention ways they feel they could support the victim.

When the small groups finish their notes, collect them and the pens/pencils (unless you plan to do Optional Activity 2 suggested on page 34). Tell the students that you will be reading their notes and will share from them in your next session together.

Concluding the Session

Gather the students in the area of the meeting room where you've posted "A Declaration of Independence from Bullying: Parts 1, 2, & 3" (Teaching Masters 3, 6, & 10). Call on one of the students to read all three parts aloud.

Then give a different student a copy of "A Declaration of Independence from Bullying: Part 4" (Teaching Master 12). Ask him or her to read it aloud to the group:

> We have discovered that bullying is a problem its victims cannot solve on their own. We realize that they need and deserve our help and the help of everyone in our school. We now declare that we say "No!" to bullying and promise to work to make our school a place where no one has to be a victim, where everyone can be a friend.

After the reading, have the student post the sheet. Then, to help the students declare their independence from bullying, invite them to suggest ideas for making friends and/or sustaining friendships.

Afterward, thank the students for their ideas. Remind them of the time of their next session, when they will discover the particular kind of help victims of bullying need to feel better, to have friends, and to be safe at school.

Optional Activities

1. If your students are keeping journals, suggest journaling questions like the following:

   • Why can't victims of bullying deal with the problem successfully on their own?

   • If you were a victim of bullying at school, what would you want the school to do for you?

   • What are some ways you could help victims of bullying feel safe at school?

2. To expand the activity in "Closing the Session," consider inviting students to sign their names to the copy of "A Declaration of Independence from Bullying: Part 4" (Teaching Master 12).

3. To help the students become more sensitive to the plight of victims of violence, consider inviting a speaker from the front lines of those dealing with violence to speak to your class; for example, someone from law enforcement, emergency medicine, counselors, a representative from a battered woman's shelter, or a victim's advocate from the court. Ask the speaker to address the victim's inability to deal with the problem on his or her own because of the inherent imbalance in bully/victim situations.

Session 5

Aim

To help the students recognize the distinction between "ratting" and "reporting" in order to get help in a bullying situation

Objectives

By the end of the session, the students will

- define both "ratting" and "reporting"

- understand the difference between "ratting" and "reporting"

- recognize that they need to tell someone they trust about bullying to get help

- appreciate how adults in their school are willing to help stop bullying

- learn their school's procedure for "reporting" bullying behavior

Materials

- the No-Bullying logo poster

- the "Bullying Happens…" poster

- the "Bullying Behaviors" poster

- copies of "Ratting Is…" (Teaching Master 13)

- copies of "Reporting Is…" (Teaching Master 14)

- copies of "Is It Bullying?" (Teaching Master 11)

- copies of "A Declaration of Independence from Bullying: Parts 1, 2, 3, & 4" (Teaching Masters 3, 6, 10, & 12)

- one copy of "A Declaration of Independence from Bullying: Part 5" (Teaching Master 15)

- chalkboard and chalk or newsprint and markers

- colored markers or colored pencils

- glue sticks or tape

- large sheets of light-colored construction paper

- pens or pencils

- slips of paper

Preparing for the Session

Carefully read through the entire plan prior to presenting the session. Make copies of "Ratting Is…" (Teaching Master 13) and "Reporting Is…" (Teaching Master 14), one for every two students. Also, make five copies of "Is It Bullying?" (Teaching Master 11), for use as in the previous session. Make one copy of "A Declaration of Independence from Bullying: Part 5" (Teaching Master 15). Arrange to have colored markers or colored pencils, a glue stick or tape, and a large sheet of light-colored construction paper for every two students. Have pens or pencils available. Cut slips of paper, one for each student. Be ready to explain the procedure your school has previously agreed upon for reporting bullying. Give some thought to using the Optional Activities, and if you choose to do so, make necessary arrangements. Check to make sure that the No-Bullying logo poster, the "Bullying Happens…" poster, and the "Bullying Behaviors" posters are displayed prominently in the meeting space.

Background for the Teacher

Given the inclination of so many in society who "just don't want to get involved," it should come as no surprise that students are unwilling to get involved in dealing with bullying when they see it happening to another. Many students believe that telling adults about bullying will only make matters worse. In fact, that perception may well be the students' experience with bully/victim conflict, especially given the far too pervasive climate of tolerance and entitlement that has long surrounded bullying.

From early training, children—even the most caring—have been advised not to tell on others and to deal with conflicts on their own. This is good advice when the conflict is between individuals equal in power. However, it is not good counsel in a bully/victim situation, because, as we have clearly seen, the victim can never win. Thinking that a victim of bullying can resolve the problem on his or her own without help is like thinking a middle school student can solve a problem in quantum physics without help.

In Session 4, the students discovered the plight of victims and learned to empathize with them. They recognized that victims of bullying cannot handle bullying on their own. If they could, *they would have done so.* Victims of bullying need help. In this session, the students realize that such help must come not only from the solidarity of students, but from the intervention of an adult. Since adults in a school cannot always be aware of all bullying, and since bullying generally does not occur in the classroom, students are encouraged to tell appropriate adults when it does occur.

Your challenge in presenting this session is to help the students recognize that it is appropriate to "report" when they are being bullied or when they witness bullying, while discouraging "ratting." An open and nonjudgmental attitude on your part will go a long way in helping students "report," not "rat."

Remember, students who are victims of bullying are afraid to tell. They fear both physical retribution and social ostracism. Make sure that all your students understand that you and all school staff are committed to protecting the victims of bullying—both from further bullying and from retribution for reporting such behavior—and that students reported for bullying will be watched and dealt with appropriately by you and others at your school, and that they will be held strictly accountable for any subsequent bullying behavior.

Session Plan

Beginning the Session

Choose from the notes the small groups wrote to victims of bullying in the previous session (see Session 4, Step 7), any messages that you feel speak well to the students' growth in empathy for the victims of bullying and/or any that are particularly insightful or notable.

Should any of the students' notes mention thoughts or ideas of revenge/aggression toward the perpetrator(s) of bullying, take time to explain that such behavior does little to end bullying. Remind the students that those who bully are excited by victims who fight back and by aggression from others who "take the victim's side." Thus aggression toward the bully will only result in producing more aggression from the bully.

Finally, if any note recommends getting help from a trusted adult, be sure to highlight that suggestion.

Leading the Session

1. Write the phrase, "It only makes matters worse when you report bullying to an adult," on the board or newsprint. Ask for a show of hands to determine how many of the students agree and how many disagree with this statement. Ask the students to share why they would or would not consider telling an adult about bullying—whether it was happening to them or they witnessed it happening to another.

   Expect some, if not most, of the students to be reluctant to believe that telling an adult is a good idea. Even if they believe that a victim of bullying can't solve the problem on his or her own, they also possess a confused sense of "fairness" that tells them, "It's wrong to rat." That is, it's inappropriate for them to tell on another student.

2. Write the word "Reporting" on the board or newsprint and the word "Ratting" next to it. Invite the students to brainstorm examples of each. Record on the board or newsprint. Then, drawing on their examples of "ratting," help the students recognize that ratting is speaking to someone about a problem:

   • just to get somebody in trouble

   • just to get their own way

   • just to make themselves look good and somebody else look bad

   Explain that when we do any of these things, we're ratting.

3. Next, point out on the board or newsprint any brainstorming examples the students gave of "reporting." Help the students see that reporting is speaking to someone they trust about a problem in order to get help for themselves or for another.

4. Divide the class into pairs. If a student is left out, pair up with him or her yourself. Tell partners they are to work together to make posters about ratting and reporting. Give each pair colored markers or colored pencils, a copy of "Ratting Is…" (Teaching Master 13), a copy of "Reporting Is…" (Teaching Master 14), a glue stick or tape, and a large sheet of light-colored construction paper. Offer the following directions:

(1) Together, agree on a definition of "ratting" and print it clearly on "Ratting Is…" (Teaching Master 13).

(2) Then, agree on a definition of "reporting" and print it clearly on "Reporting Is…" (Teaching Master 14).

(3) Add color to the illustrations on both teaching masters, then use the glue stick or tape to mount both on the large sheet of construction paper, leaving enough room at the bottom of the sheet to write a brief slogan.

(4) Finally, devise a brief slogan that *encourages reporting bullying behavior* and print it clearly on the bottom of the poster.

When the students finish, encourage partners to share their posters with the class.

To complete the activity, have partners write their names on the back of their posters. Then collect the posters along with the colored markers or pencils and the paste or glue sticks. Tell the students that you will arrange to hang their posters throughout the school.

5. Remind the students how they learned that victims of bullying have the deck stacked against them. Tell them that victims need help and support in order to put an end to the bullying. Emphasize that the best way to help is for the rest of us to stand together against bullying and to *report all such behavior to a trusted adult in our school*. Say:

> "If you report any bullying you see or know about, you give power to the victim of bullying and help him or her get help."

6. Go on to outline for the students the procedure your school has previously agreed upon for reporting bullying (e.g., *how* they are to report, *to whom* they are to report, *when and where* they are to report, etc.). Make sure the students understand that when they "report" bullying, their anonymity will be insured, re-emphasizing that an adult *will* step in to help and protect.

7. To practice using the school's procedures of "telling/reporting" to get help, divide the class into the same five small groups they were in during Session 4. Give each group a copy of "Is It Bullying?" (Teaching Master 11) used in Session 4. Assign each group to one of the bullying scenarios (1, 2, 4, 6, and 9). Ask small group members to imagine that they have witnessed or otherwise know about the bullying described in their scenario. Direct each small group to use its scenario to develop a role play that

shows the right way to get help for the person who is the victim of bullying. Give the groups a few minutes to devise their role plays. Then allow two to three minutes for each role play. After each presentation, take a moment to process it and to correct any misconceptions.

Afterward, be sure to compliment the students on their insights and cooperative work.

Concluding the Session

Gather the students in the area of the meeting room where you've posted "A Declaration of Independence from Bullying: Parts 1, 2, 3, & 4" (Teaching Masters 3, 6, 10, & 12). Call on one of the students to read all four parts aloud.

Then give a different student a copy of "A Declaration of Independence from Bullying: Part 5" (Teaching Master 15). Ask him or her to read it aloud to the group:

> We have come to appreciate that ending bullying means trusting one another. We trust that the adults in our school are willing and able to help us stop bullying. We now declare that we say "No!" to bullying and commit ourselves to reporting it, so that everyone in our school will feel safe.

After the reading, have the student post the sheet. Make sure all the students have pens or pencils. Distribute slips of paper. Then, to help the students become more independent of bullying, have them write on the slip one thing that would help them feel more safe at school. When the students finish writing, collect the slips and share randomly some (those that are appropriate) with the class. Finally, collect pens/pencils (unless you decide to do Optional Activity 4 suggested on page 41).

As you dismiss the students, remind them of their next, and final, meeting time. Tell them that at that session the principal will join them to explain how the school will deal with those who bully.

Optional Activities

1. If your students are keeping journals, suggest journaling questions like the following:

   • What, if anything, makes you fearful of reporting bullying?

   • Do you really think telling a trusted adult about bullying can help?

- If you were a victim of bullying and were afraid to report it, would you want someone who knew about it to report it? Why or why not?

2. To enhance Step 5, create a "Reporting Bullying Sheet" to give each student as a reminder of your school's procedure for reporting bullying. Simply outline the procedure and have it duplicated on easy-to-carry sheets or index cards that the students can keep with them.

3. To extend Step 7, consider arranging to have your class present all or some of these role plays to children in the lower grades in order to give them appropriate examples of "reporting/telling" to get help.[1]

4. To expand the activity in "Concluding the Session," consider inviting students to sign their names to the copy of "A Declaration of Independence from Bullying: Part 5" (Teaching Master 15).

---

[1] If yours is a separate Middle School, arrange to present the role plays to children in a neighboring Elementary School that is also engaged in the *No-Bullying Program.* If your middle school students are part of a K–8 school, simply present the role plays to children in the lower grades.

Session 6

Aim

To present school-wide consequences for engaging in bullying behaviors

Objectives

By the end of the session, the students will

- understand that bullying behavior is not to be tolerated in their school

- discover that engaging in bullying will bring swift consequences

- know the school-wide consequences for bullying

- better understand that all adults in the school are committed to making the school a safe and secure place

Materials

- the No-Bullying logo poster

- the "Bullying Happens…" poster

- the "Bullying Behaviors" poster

- copies of "A Declaration of Independence from Bullying: Parts 1, 2, 3, 4, & 5" (Teaching Masters 3, 6, 10, 12, & 15)

- copies of "When There's No Bullying Here…" (Teaching Master 16)

- one copy of "A Declaration of Independence from Bullying: Part 6" (Teaching Master 17)

- copies of "Our Declaration of Independence from Bullying" (Teaching Master 18)

- chalkboard and chalk or newsprint and marker

- posterboard or newsprint and markers

- tape

- scissors

- pens or pencils

- optional: index cards

Preparing for the Session

Carefully read through the session plan in advance. Prior to the session, use a marker and posterboard or newsprint to make a large poster entitled "Bullying Consequences." With the aid and consensus of school staff, list your school's consequences for engaging in bullying behaviors. Arrange to have the principal in attendance to present the core of the session. Make copies of "When There's No Bullying Here…" (Teaching Master 16), at least two copies per student. Make one copy of "A Declaration of Independence from Bullying: Part 6" (Teaching Master 17). Make copies of "Our Declaration of Independence from Bullying" (Teaching Master 18), one for each student. Make sure each student has access to a pen or pencil and a pair of scissors.

> **Note:** "When There's No Bullying Here…" (Teaching Master 16) is a two-sided worksheet. If you do not have access to a copier that is capable of producing two-sided copies, you will need to make copies of each side of the Teaching Master and then carefully glue them back-to-back. To facilitate this process, check with your school's art department to see if spray glue or spray fixative is available.

Carefully consider using the Optional Activities. See to it that the No-Bullying logo poster and the "Bullying Happens…" and "Bullying Behaviors" posters are displayed prominently in the meeting space.

Background for the Teacher

Students in middle school generally have little difficulty in understanding the concept of consequences. Unfortunately, many children have experienced how consequences are not fairly applied. They need powerful reassurance that your school has no tolerance whatsoever for bullying and that your school will impose swift and strict consequences when it does occur. *Trust* is what is at stake here. The students need to trust that responsible and caring adults will intervene in bullying behavior and keep them safe.

Since research has shown that many students do not believe that adults can help them deal with bullying, it becomes your task to begin to change that perception. Thus it may be appropriate for you—or the principal, who will be presenting the core of this session—to assure the students that adults in your school have had some training and have learned new information about dealing with bullying.

Session Plan

Beginning the Session

Invite the school principal to join with the students as they gather in a circle. Tell the students that the principal will be a visitor to their class today. Draw attention to the copy of the No-Bullying logo poster. Ask the students to explain its purpose.

Go on to ask one of the students to read aloud the definition of bullying on the "Bullying Happens…" poster. Then, pointing out a few of the behaviors listed on that poster and on the "Bullying Behaviors" poster, ask volunteers to explain how someone who is a victim of that behavior would feel.

Next, invite the students to recall the difference between ratting and reporting. Ask:

> What's the difference between ratting and reporting? (Look for responses indicating that *ratting gets someone* into *trouble; reporting gets someone* out of *trouble.*)

Take time to correct any misunderstandings.

Finally, have the students explain how they could help themselves or someone else who is being bullied by *telling* a trusted adult.

Leading the Session

1. Have the students brainstorm the word "Consequences." Record ideas on the board or newsprint. Afterward, ask the students to offer examples of "consequences" for certain types of behavior. For example, you might ask:

   • What's a consequence in your home for breaking curfew?

   • What's a consequence in school for cheating on a test?

- What's a consequence of being a friend to someone?

- What's a consequence of playing your best during a game of soccer?

Also encourage the students to share personal examples of consequences. Again, record ideas and comments on the board or newsprint.

Note: Save these ideas and comments for use later in the session (see Step 4 below).

After the students respond, go on to tell them that their principal is going to talk to them about the consequences of engaging in bullying behavior in their school.

2. The school principal will now address the students about your school's no-tolerance rule about bullying and about the consequences of engaging in bullying behavior. Make sure the principal has access to the "Bullying Consequences" poster you prepared prior to the session. The principal should also take time to reassure the students that school staff will support and protect victims of bullying.

3. When the principal completes his or her presentation, have the students post the "Bullying Consequences" poster in their classroom. Then, using the poster, briefly review the list of consequences, checking for understanding and letting the students know that you—and all the other adults in the school—agree with the consequences, promise to be supportive to students who report bullying and want to end it in their school, and pledge to protect all victims of bullying.

4. Draw attention to the board or newsprint on which are catalogued the students' examples of consequences (see Step 1 above). Point out that not all consequences are negative (or punitive) ones. For example, the consequence of playing one's best during a game of soccer may be winning the game or feeling a sense of pride; the consequence of being a friend to someone might be getting a loyal friend in return. Ask the students to offer examples of "positive" consequences for caring behavior. Add the students' ideas to the consequences list on the board or newsprint.

5. Challenge the students to develop their own plans for making their school a safer and more caring place. Possibilities include providing more supervision in areas where bullying occurs—bathrooms, halls, locker rooms, etc. Encourage the students to find solutions to one specific problem they are experiencing.

Afterward, go on to propose that the students devise a list of "positive" consequences to be applied by the school for those who engage in the opposite of bullying behavior, *caring behavior*; for example, depending upon the age of the student(s) "caught caring," some sort of special recognition, an award certificate, a privilege, a prize, etc. Encourage the students to be realistic in their planning, being sure to develop simple and specific ways to implement their ideas.

6. Distribute scissors and copies of the two-sided Teaching Master, "When There's No Bullying Here…" (Teaching Master 16). Point out the text at the top of Side 1 and ask one of the students to read it aloud. Then have the students turn to Side 2 and read the directions with them. Allow the students to work on their own in completing their puzzles. However, you may want to circulate and offer help where needed. Likewise, if you made one of the puzzles prior to the session, you can show it to the students as a completed example.

When all the students have finished making their puzzles, have them use them as directed and together discover the positive consequences of ending bullying in school. Then have them open the puzzle to find out what our saying "No!" to bullying means for them and their school.

Point out to the students that the easiest way to end bullying in their school is to remember what C.A.R.E. is:

> **C**onsequences for bullying
>
> **A**dult intervention
>
> **R**eport all bullying
>
> **E**mpathy for victims

7. Hand out additional copies of "When There's No Bullying Here…" (Teaching Master 16) and allow the students to make puzzles to present to students in lower grades.[2] Now that the students have made their own puzzles, making extras should go rather quickly. Arrange a time for your students to present the completed puzzles to the younger students.

---

[2] If yours is a separate Middle School, arrange to present the puzzles to children in a neighboring Elementary School, preferably—but not necessarily—one that is also engaged in the *No-Bullying Program*. If your middle school students are part of a K–8 school, simply present the puzzles to children in the lower grades.

Concluding the Session

Gather the students in the area of the meeting room where you've posted "A Declaration of Independence from Bullying: Parts 1, 2, 3, 4, & 5" (Teaching Masters 3, 6, 10, 12, & 15). Call on one of the students to read all five parts aloud.

Then give a different student a copy of "A Declaration of Independence from Bullying: Part 6" (Teaching Master 17). Ask him or her to read it aloud to the group:

> We accept and agree with our school's consequences for bullying, for we realize that when one of us suffers from bullying, all of us are hurt. As we declare our independence from bullying, we also declare our dependence on one another, and we acknowledge that saying "No!" to bullying in our school means saying "Yes!" to caring.

After the reading, have the student post the sheet. Make sure all the students all have pens. Then invite them to declare their independence from bullying by saying:

> "If you are you willing to acknowledge that saying 'No!' to bullying in our school means saying 'Yes!' to caring for one another, please come forward and sign your name."

As the students sign the sheet, thank them for their commitment, and give each one a copy of "Our Declaration of Independence from Bullying" (Teaching Master 18), which contains the "declaration" in its entirety.

Collect pens (unless you plan to use Optional Activities listed below) and all other extraneous materials.

Before you dismiss the students, be sure to thank them for all their hard work, their willingness to put an end to bullying in their school, and their commitment to C.A.R.E.

Optional Activities

1. If your students are keeping journals, suggest completing journal entries like the following:

   • What I liked best about the No-Bullying Program was…

   • This is how I would change/improve this program…

   • I think the No-Bullying Program made (or did not make) a difference in our school because…

Tell the students that as they review their journals, and if they feel strongly that their insights could contribute to making their school a safer place, you would be open to hearing their thoughts and ideas in private.

2. To help the students remember the "Bullying Consequences," have them copy the consequences on an index card that they can keep and carry with them.

3. To extend and enhance Steps 6 and 7, have the students make C.A.R.E. buttons to wear and share with other students in their school.

4. Consider making an extra copy of "Our Declaration of Independence from Bullying" (Teaching Master 18) and having all the students sign it. Then arrange to frame it and hang it in a permanent place in the school, e.g., near the main bulletin board or in the school's trophy case.

Teaching Masters

1. No-Bullying Logo Poster

2. No-Bullying Logos

3. A Declaration of Independence from Bullying: Part 1

4. Bullying Happens…

5. What's Happening?

6. A Declaration of Independence from Bullying: Part 2

7. 20 Statements

8. The Bully/Victim Characteristics Chart

9. The Bully/Victim Characteristics Grid

10. A Declaration of Independence from Bullying: Part 3

11. Is It Bullying?

12. A Declaration of Independence from Bullying: Part 4

13. Ratting Is…

14. Reporting Is…

15. A Declaration of Independence from Bullying: Part 5

16. When There's No Bullying Here…

17. A Declaration of Independence from Bullying: Part 6

18. Our Declaration of Independence from Bullying

19. Bullying Behavior Chart

20. Feelings List

We, the generation that will be adults in the twenty-first century, in order to grow to be our best selves and to shape a future free of abuse, declare our independence from bullying by saying "No!" to bullying in our school.

BULLYING HAPPENS...
when someone with *greater* power
unfairly hurts someone
with *less* power
over and over again.

_____   _____   _____

Power   **Power**   **Power**

What's Happening?

1. I am a…
   - ❏ Girl ❏ Boy

2. I get bullied at school by being pushed, kicked, or hit.
   - ❏ Never ❏ Once in awhile ❏ A lot ❏ Every day

3. I get bullied at school by name-calling, put-downs, teasing, or being left out.
   - ❏ Never ❏ Once in awhile ❏ A lot ❏ Every day

4. I bully others at school.
   - ❏ Never ❏ Once in awhile ❏ A lot ❏ Every day

5. I think that most of the bullying that happens at our school happens…
   - ❏ in classrooms
   - ❏ in hallways
   - ❏ on the school grounds
   - ❏ in the bathrooms
   - ❏ in the cafeteria
   - ❏ on the school bus

6. I get bullied on my way to and from school.
   - ❏ Never ❏ Once in awhile ❏ A lot ❏ Every day

7. When I'm in school, I worry about being bullied.
   - ❏ Never ❏ Once in awhile ❏ A lot ❏ Every day

8. If someone bullies me, I usually
   - ❏ Fight back
   - ❏ Tell the bully to stop
   - ❏ Don't do anything
   - ❏ Tell my parents
   - ❏ Get revenge
   - ❏ Tell another student
   - ❏ Tell an adult at school
   - ❏ I don't get bullied

9. If I see someone else getting bullied, I usually
   - ❏ Help the victim
   - ❏ Tell an adult at school
   - ❏ Tell my parents
   - ❏ Join in the bullying
   - ❏ Tell another student
   - ❏ Don't do anything

10. To help me feel safe at our school, I think adults should
    - ❏ Make rules about bullying
    - ❏ Enforce rules about bullying
    - ❏ Teach more lessons about how to get along better
    - ❏ Have better supervision of:
      - ❏ school bus
      - ❏ school grounds
      - ❏ cafeteria
      - ❏ bathrooms
      - ❏ hallways
      - ❏ classrooms

On the back of this survey, write anything else you think your teacher should know about bullying in your school.

We recognize that bullying is an abuse of power whose negative effects fill our school with fear. We now declare that we say "No!" to bullying and promise to work to make our school a place where no one has to be afraid.

20 Statements

Read each of the following statements. If you think the statement is true, mark it with a **T**. If you think it's false, mark it with an **F**.

Kids who bully others...

1. _____ usually feel guilty about their behavior.

2. _____ don't really feel compassion for others.

3. _____ are boys only. Girls don't bully.

4. _____ are loners.

5. _____ may feel secure and have high self-image.

6. _____ do not really mean to hurt others.

7. _____ feel that their victims deserve to be bullied.

8. _____ usually do okay in school work.

9. _____ will back off if their victims fight back.

10. _____ always win.

Kids who are victims of bullying...

1. _____ usually get what they deserve.

2. _____ feel secure and have high self-image.

3. _____ are loners.

4. _____ sometimes provoke the bullying.

5. _____ should fight back.

6. _____ cry easily.

7. _____ spend a lot of time and energy being afraid.

9. _____ never carry weapons for protection.

10 _____ always lose.

The Bully/Victim Characteristics Chart

Kids who bully...

- are excited by their bullying behavior.
- enjoy feelings of power and control.
- lack compassion and empathy for their victims.
- enjoy causing pain.
- are calm and show little emotion.
- blame the victims.
- think that the innocent remarks or actions of others are meant to hurt them.
- are usually average students.
- do not have low self-esteem.
- usually have a small network of friends.
- are successful at hiding their bullying behavior.
- are excited by their victims' reactions such as fighting back.
- who are boys more often use physical force, insults, and threats.
- who are girls more often rely on social alienation and intimidation, such as excluding their victims, threatening them, or making them feel as if they don't belong.

There are two types of victims: Passive and Provocative.

Kids who are *passive* victims...

- show a lot of emotion.
- rarely tell about being bullied, because they think it will make matters worse, and they don't think adults can help.
- may carry weapons for protection.
- do not encourage attack; they don't "ask for it."
- are sensitive, cry easily, and are easy to pick on.
- may be shy and lacking in social skills.
- are usually insecure and lacking in self-esteem.
- are usually chosen last or left out.
- may appear to lack humor.
- have few or no friends.

- are often anxious and easily upset.
- are bullied repeatedly.
- may use money or toys (as bribes) for protection.

Kids who are *provocative* victims...

- are pesky and repeatedly irritate others.
- are quick-tempered and prone to fight back.
- get others charged up.
- may be clumsy, immature, restless.
- provoke bullying; they "egg on" kids who bully.
- sometimes look as if they are bullies themselves, but, unlike true bullies, they always lose in the end.

The Bully/Victim Characteristic Grid

	Group 1	Group 2	Group 3	Group 4
Bully Characteristics				
Excited by his/her bullying behavior				
Enjoys causing pain				
Blames the victim(s)				
Has a small group of friends				
Successfully hides his/her bullying				
Passive Victim Characteristics				
In some way is not as powerful as the bully				
Doesn't tell about being bullied				
Is sensitive; cries easily				
Rarely fights back				
Does not invite attack				
Provocative Victim Characteristics				
Irritates the bully				
Quick-tempered; fights back				
Seems immature or uncoordinated				
In some way is not as powerful as the bully				
May appear to be a bully, but never wins				

We understand that bullying is isolating. It separates us, turning us into perpetrators and victims and observers. It shatters community and changes "all of us" to "them and us." We now declare that we say "No!" to bullying and promise to work to make our school a place where no one has to feel left out.

Is It Bullying?

Read each of the following scenarios. Decide whether each describes bullying or not. Mark **Y** for "Yes," **N** for "No."

1. _____ John, who is large for his age, repeatedly follows Steve around, teasing and making fun of him.

2. _____ Betty, one of the "In crowd," has been spreading rumors about Janine around school. Janine is now spending her lunch periods alone.

3. _____ Sean and Julio are the same age and size. Sean pushes Julio in the hallway.

4. _____ Annie continually calls Adrianne on the telephone at night and says things like, "You better watch it at school."

5. _____ Danielle and Maria have gone to school together since kindergarten. All of a sudden, Maria starts calling Danielle names.

6. _____ Every time he sees him in school, Ron, an eighth grader, punches Ted, a sixth grader, in the arm.

7. _____ Damon and Pat are seventh graders who end up wrestling on the school grounds every day.

8. _____ Sally a tall seventh grader, accidentally bumped into Sue, a very short sixth grader, knocking her down.

9. _____ Max and his friends make a game out of tormenting Felicia. Now Max tells Felicia that he wants to meet her at the school dance and go out for pizza afterward. However, Max doesn't plan to show up at the dance. Max tells his buddies to laugh at Felicia when she shows up at the dance without him.

10. _____ Jonah and Ralph are in the same homeroom. Every day they swipe each others' baseball caps.

We have discovered that bullying is a problem its victims cannot solve on their own. We realize that they need and deserve our help and the help of everyone in our school. We now declare that we say "No!" to bullying and promise to work to make our school a place where no one has to be a victim, where everyone can be a friend.

Ratting Is…

Reporting Is...

We have come to appreciate that ending bullying means trusting one another. We trust that the adults in our school are willing and able to help us stop bullying. We now declare that we say "No!" to bullying and commit ourselves to reporting it, so that everyone in our school will feel safe.

Follow the directions on the Side 2 of this sheet to unravel a puzzle about what the consequences can be if we end bullying in our school.

In Our School...

No Has T Afr

"No!" To

One o Be aid

To Bullying

yone eel e

Ever Can Fri

Bullying

Means "Yes!" To

es Wil Eve

end A eB yone

Consequences for bullying
Adult intervention
Report all bullying
Empathy for victims

If We

One Feel Out

No Has To Left

Say "No!"

Directions: Cut along the dotted line to make a square. Along the solid lines, fold in the four corners to the dot at the center of the square. Turn the square over. Again, along the solid lines, fold in the four corners to the center of the square. Fold the square in half, top to bottom. Open. Then fold the square in half, side-to-side. Insert thumbs and forefingers under the square's flaps and push together. Move fingers back and forth to discover what the consequences can be if we end bullying in our school. Open the puzzle to find out what our saying "No!" to bullying means for you and our school.

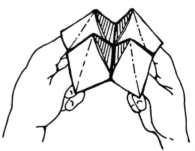

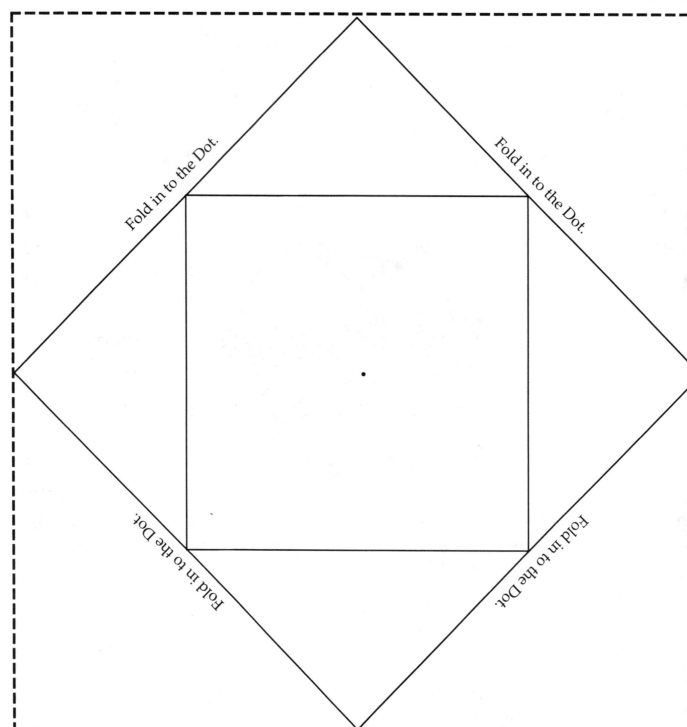

Fold in to the Dot.

Fold in to the Dot.

Fold in to the Dot.

Fold in to the Dot.

We accept and agree with our school's consequences for bullying, for we realize that when one of us suffers from bullying, all of us are hurt. As we declare our independence from bullying, we also declare our dependence on one another, and we acknowledge that saying "No!" to bullying in our school means saying "Yes!" to caring.

Our Declaration of Independence from Bullying

We, the generation that will be adults in the twenty-first century, in order to grow to be our best selves and to shape a future free of abuse, declare our independence from bullying by saying "No!" to bullying in our school.

We recognize that bullying is an abuse of power whose negative effects fill our school with fear. We now declare that we say "No!" to bullying and promise to work to make our school a place where no one has to be afraid.

We understand that bullying is isolating. It separates us, turning us into perpetrators and victims and observers. It shatters community and changes "all of us" to "them and us." We now declare that we say "No!" to bullying and promise to work to make our school a place where no one has to feel left out.

We have discovered that bullying is a problem its victims cannot solve on their own. We realize that they need and deserve our help and the help of everyone in our school. We now declare that we say "No!" to bullying and promise to work to make our school a place where no one has to be a victim, where everyone can be a friend.

We have come to appreciate that ending bullying means trusting one another. We trust that the adults in our school are willing and able to help us stop bullying. We now declare that we say "No!" to bullying and commit ourselves to reporting it, so that everyone in our school will feel safe.

We accept and agree with our school's consequences for bullying, for we realize that when one of us suffers from bullying, all of us are hurt. As we declare our independence from bullying, we also declare our dependence on one another, and we acknowledge that saying "No!" to bullying in our school means saying "Yes!" to caring.

Bullying Behavior Chart

| Physical | | Emotional | | Social | |
| Harm to another's body or property | | Harm to another's self-esteem | | Harm to another's group acceptance | |
verbal	non-verbal	verbal	non-verbal	verbal	non-verbal
Taunting Expressing physical superiority	Making threatening gestures Defacing property Pushing/shoving Taking small items from others	Insulting remarks Calling names Teasing about possessions, clothes	Giving dirty looks Holding nose or other insulting gestures Saying someone has germs or is unclean	Gossiping Starting/spreading rumors Teasing publicly about clothes, looks, etc…	Passively not including in group Playing mean tricks
Threatening physical harm Blaming victim	Damaging property Stealing Initiating fights Scratching Tripping or causing a fall Assaulting	Insulting family Harassing with phone calls Insulting intelligence, athletic ability, etc…	Defacing school work Falsifying school work Defacing personal property, clothing, etc…	Insulting race, gender Increasing gossip/rumors Undermining other relationships	Making someone look foolish Excluding from the group
Making repeated and/or graphic threats Practicing extortion Making threats to secure silence: "If you tell, I will…"	Destroying property Setting fires Biting Physical cruelty Making repeated, violent threats Assaulting with a weapon	Frightening with phone calls Challenging in public	Ostracizing Destroying personal property or clothing	Threatening total group exclusion	Arranging public humiliation Total group rejection/ostracizing

Bullying involves exploitation of a less powerful person. There must be an unfair advantage being exerted. Bully/victim conflict is best understood as a dynamic relationship. Whether or not a behavior is bullying depends on its effect upon the victim. This chart was designed to assist with the identification of bullying behavior in situations where an unfair advantage exists. The seriousness for all levels of behavior should be evaluated based on the harm to the victim and the frequency of the occurrences.

Feelings List

Do you know what? "Good" or "bad," "right" or "wrong" are not names of feelings. Nope. They're judgment calls about feelings. Feelings aren't "good" or "bad," "right" or "wrong." Feelings just are. It's okay to feel the way you feel. However, it's not always easy to name what you're feeling. But you can do something about that. You can expand your feelings inventory. Here's a list of feeling words to help you recognize and identify the feelings you're having.

afraid	embarrassed	insecure	restless
aggressive	enthusiastic	inspired	sad
alone	envious	jealous	safe
amused	excited	joyful	sorry
angry	exhausted	left out	stupid
anxious	foolish	lonely	tense
appreciated	frightened	loved	tired
bitter	frustrated	miserable	uncertain
bored	furious	nervous	unloved
concerned	glad	panicky	wanted
confused	guilty	peaceful	worried
contented	heartbroken	powerful/less	worthless
delighted	hopeful	proud	worthwhile
depressed	hopeless	rejected	
disappointed	hurt	relaxed	
discouraged	impatient	relieved	

Wow! Quite the list! And there are many other feeling words, too. See if you can add four more feeling words here.

_____ _____ _____ _____

Additional Resources

The following materials are available from the Johnson Institute. Call us at 800-231-5165 for ordering information, current prices, or a complete listing of Johnson Institute resources.

No-Bullying Program Materials

Tee shirts with the No-Bullying logo displayed on the front, posters, stickers, and extra teaching manuals for your school may be ordered simply by calling the sales department at Johnson Institute.

Video Programs

An Attitude Adjustment for Ramie. 15 minutes. Order #V429

Anger: Handle It Before It Handles You. 15 minutes. Order #V450

Broken Toy. 30 minutes. Order #V462

Choices & Consequences. 33 minutes. Order #V400

Conflict: Think About It, Talk About It, Try to Work It Out. 15 minutes. Order #V451

Dealing with Anger: A Violence Prevention Program for African-American Youth. 52 minutes (males), 68 minutes (females). Order #V433 (for males); Order #V456 (for females)

Double Bind. 15 minutes. Order #V430

Good Intentions, Bad Results. 30 minutes. Order #V440

It's Not Okay to Bully. 15 minutes. Order #5883JH

Peer Mediation: Conflict Resolution in Schools. 28 minutes. Order #V458Kit

Respect & Protect: A Solution to Stopping Violence in Schools and Communities. 28 minutes. Order #V460

Tulip Doesn't Feel Safe. 12 minutes. Order #V438

Publications

Bosch, Carl W. *Bully on the Bus.* Order #P413

Boyd, Lizi. *Bailey the Big Bully.* Order #P422

Carlson, Nancy. *Loudmouth George and the Sixth Grade Bully.* Order #P414

Crary, Elizabeth. *I Can't Wait.* Order #P431

———. *I'm Furious.* Order #P506

———. *I'm Mad.* Order #P509

———. *I Want It.* Order #P427

———. *My Name Is Not Dummy.* Order #P429

Cummings, Carol. *I'm Always in Trouble.* Order #P418

———. *Sticks and Stones.* Order #P420

———. *Tattlin' Madeline.* Order #P421

———. *Win, Win Day.* Order #P419

Davis, Diane. *Working with Children from Violent Homes: Ideas and Techniques.* Order #P244

DeMarco, John. *Peer Helping Skills Program for Training Peer Helpers and Peer Tutors.* Order #P320Kit

Estes, Eleanor. *The Hundred Dresses.* Order #P411

Fleming, Martin. *Conducting Support Groups for Students Affected by Chemical Dependence: A Guide for Educators and Other Professionals.* Order #P020

Freeman, Shelley MacKay. *From Peer Pressure to Peer Support: Alcohol and other Drug Prevention Through Group Process.* Order #P147-7-8 (for grades 7, 8); Order #P147-9-10 (for grades 9, 10); Order #P147-11-12 (for grades 11, 12)

Garbarino, James, et al. *Children in Danger.* Order #P330

Goldstein, Arnold P., et al. *Aggression Replacement Training: A Comprehensive Intervention for Aggressive Youth.* Order #P329

Haven, Kendall. *Getting Along.* Order #P412

Johnsen, Karen. *The Trouble with Secrets.* Order #P425

Johnson Institute's No-Bullying Program for Grades K–Middle School. Order #546Kit

Julik, Edie. *Sailing Through the Storm to the Ocean of Peace.* Order #P437

Lawson, Ann. *Kids & Gangs: What Parents and Educators Need to Know.* Order #P322

Mills, Lauren A. *The Rag Coat.* Order #P417

Moe, Jerry, and Peter Ways, M.D. *Conducting Support Groups for Elementary Children K–6.* Order #P123

Olofsdotter, Marie. *Frej the Fearless.* Order #P438

Perry, Kate, and Charlotte Firmin. *Being Bullied.* Order #P416

Peterson, Julie, and Rebecca Janke. *Peacemaker® Program.* Order #P447

Potter-Effron, Ron. *How to Control Your Anger (Before It Controls You): A Guide for Teenagers.* Order #P277

Remboldt, Carole. *Solving Violence Problems in Your School: Why a Systematic Approach Is Necessary.* Order #P336

———. *Violence in Schools: The Enabling Factor.* Order #P337

Remboldt, Carole, and Richard Zimman. *Respect & Protect®: A Practical Step-By-StepViolence Prevention and Intervention Program for Schools and Communities.* Order #P404

Sanders, Mark. *Preventing Gang Violence in Your School.* Order #P403

Saunders, Carol Silverman. *Safe at School: Awareness and Action for Parents of Kids in Grades K–12.* Order #P340

Schaefer, Dick. *Choices & Consequences: What to Do When a Teenager Uses Alcohol/Drugs.* Order #P096

Schmidt, Teresa. *Anger Management and Violence Prevention: A Group Activities Manual for Middle and High School Students.* Order #P278

———. *Changing Families: A Group Activities Manual for Middle and High School Students.* Order #P317

———. *Daniel the Dinosaur Learns to Stand Tall Against Bullies. A Group Activities Manual to Teach K–6 Children How to Handle Other Children's Aggressive Behavior.* Order #P559

———. *Trevor and Tiffany, the Tyrannosaurus Twins, Learn to Stop Bullying. A Group Activities Manual to Teach K–6 Children How to Replace Aggressive Behavior with Assertive Behavior.* Order #P558

Schmidt, Teresa, and Thelma Spencer. *Della the Dinosaur Talks About Violence and Anger Management.* Order #P161

Schott, Sue. *Everyone Can Be Your Friend.* Order #P435

Stine, Megan, and H. William Stine. *How I Survived 5th Grade.* Mahwah, NJ: Troll Associates, 1992. Order #P415

Vernon, Ann. *Thinking, Feeling, Behaving.* (for grades 1–6) Order #P250

Villaume, Philip G., and R. Michael Foley. *Teachers at Risk: Crisis in the Classroom.* Order #P401

Wilmes, David. *Parenting for Prevention: How to Raise a Child to Say No to Alcohol/Drugs.* Order #P071

———. *Parenting for Prevention: A Parent Education Curriculum—Raising a Child to Say No to Alcohol and Other Drugs.* Order #PO72T